Fact Finders®

Kids' Translations

WITHDRAWN

THE
STAR-SPANGLED
BANNER
in Translation
What It Really Means

Revised Edition

by Elizabeth Raum

Consultant:
Holt Merchant, Professor of History
Washington and Lee University
Lexington, Virginia

CAPSTONE PRESS
a capstone imprint

Fact Finders is published by Capstone Press,
1710 Roe Crest Drive, North Mankato, Minnesota 56003.
www.mycapstone.com

Library of Congress Cataloging-in-Publication Data is available on the Library of Congress Website

ISBN: 978-1-5157-9134-8 (revised hardcover)
ISBN: 978-1-5157-6274-4 (revised paperback)
ISBN: 978-1-5157-6272-0 (ebook pdf)

Editorial Credits
Megan Schoeneberger, editor; Gene Bentdahl, set designer and illustrator; Wanda Winch, photo researcher

Photo Credits
Bridgeman Images: Photo © GraphicaArtis, 9 Bottom
Capstone Studio: Karon Dubke, Cover Bottom, 9 Top, 13 Right, 28 Left
Fusiliers' Museum, Lancashire: 20
Getty Images: Bettmann, 12 Bottom, 21
Library of Congress: 4 Right, 6 Top, 7 Top, 8 Left, 8 Right, 10 Top, 16 Right, 23, 24 Top, 24 Bottom, Harris & Ewing Collection, 17 Top, 22
North Wind Picture Archives: Cover Top, 10 Bottom, 18, 19, Gerry Embleton, 16 Left
Shutterstock: Chris Loneragan, 13 Left, dlsphotos, 25, Jose Gil, 4 Left
The Maryland Historical Society: Broadside 1814/provided by MdHS/Courtesy of the Maryland Historical Society, 7 Bottom, CA684/provided by MdHS/Courtesy of the Maryland Historical Society, 17 Bottom
The New York Public Library: The Miriam and Ira D. Wallach Division of Art, Prints and Photographs/Print Collection/ Bower, John, 14
U.S. Department of Interior: National Park Service/Adams National Historical Park, 11 Bottom

Note: Essential content terms are **bold** and are defined at the bottom of the page where they first appear.

Printed and bound in the United States of America.
010399F17

Table of Contents

CHAPTER 1

The Star-Spangled Banner

America's Song

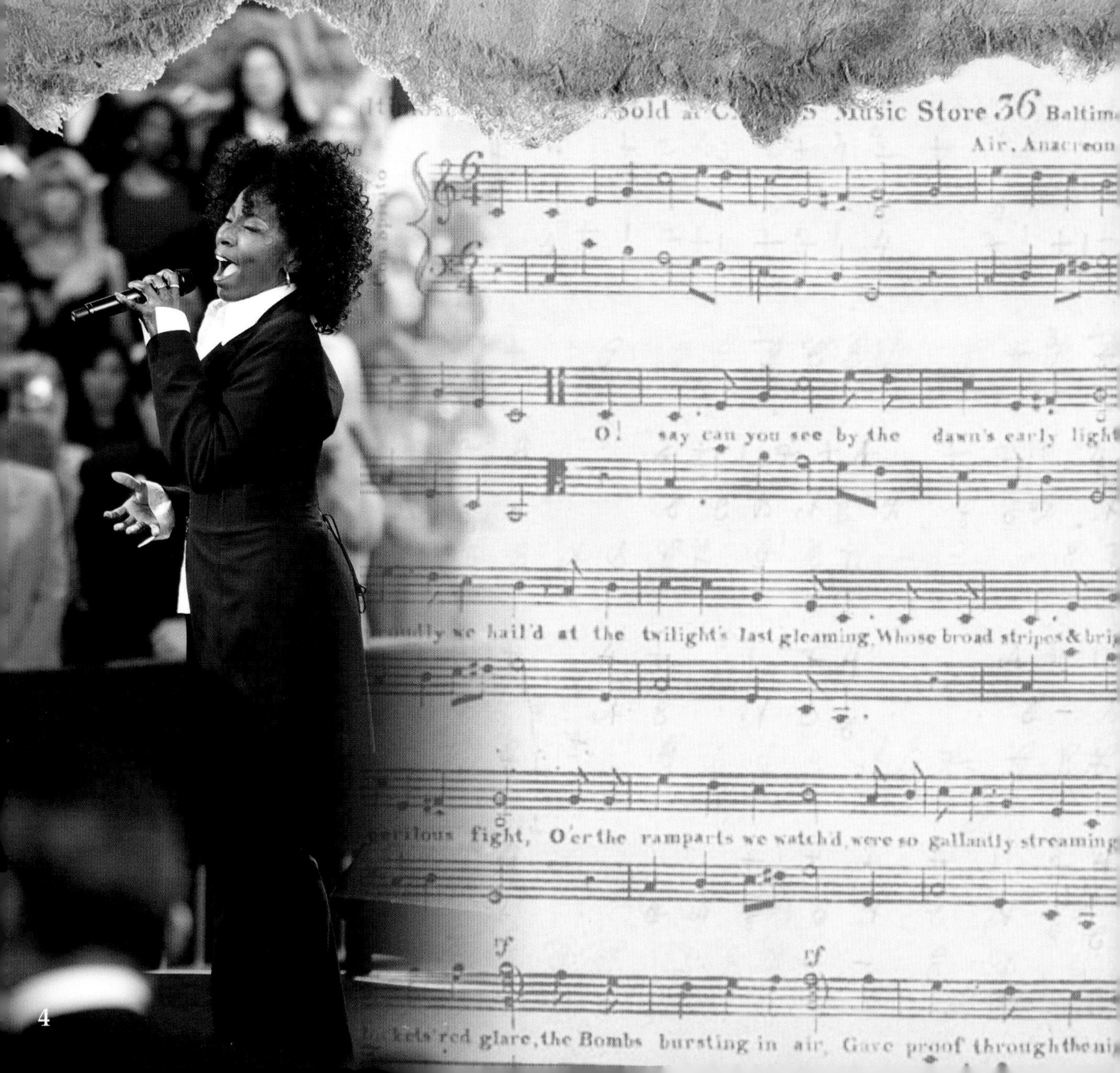

At the start of most U.S. baseball games, fans hear a similar announcement. "Ladies and Gentlemen," a voice booms over the loudspeaker. "Please rise for the singing of your national **anthem**." Everyone stands and turns toward the flag. People remove their hats. You place your hand over your heart. The first notes of the anthem float in the air. And you begin to sing.

Before you know it, the song is over. The crowd cheers wildly, and the players take the field. In the excitement, you don't even think about the song you just sang.

But "The Star-**Spangled** Banner" isn't about baseball. It doesn't really have anything to do with sports. "The Star-Spangled Banner" is the national anthem, and citizens sing it because they're proud of America.

anthem — a theme song

spangle — a bright decoration

A Yankee Doodle Don't

For its first 150 years, America didn't have a national anthem. There were several patriotic songs. "Yankee Doodle" was a particular favorite. Americans sang it with pride. But the silly lyrics were actually written by a British doctor as an insult to Americans. The lyrics weren't proper for a national anthem.

"The Star-Spangled Banner" celebrates an American victory against Great Britain during the War of 1812 (1812–1815). It honors America as the "land of the free and the home of the brave." In 1931, Congress finally made "The Star-Spangled Banner" America's official national anthem.

You probably learned the words in school. But do you know what they mean? Let's take a closer look at "The Star-Spangled Banner" to see why it was a good choice for America's national anthem.

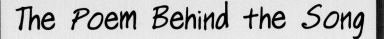

Francis Scott Key

The Poem Behind the Song

Before it was a song, "The Star-Spangled Banner" was a poem called "Defence of Fort McHenry" by Francis Scott Key. Key spent the night of September 13–14, 1814, in a boat in Chesapeake Bay, off the coast of Maryland. Key watched a battle between British ships and American soldiers at Fort McHenry. For the entire rainy night, Key heard constant gunfire and cannon blasts. Then a deathly quiet fell over the bay. In the darkness, he couldn't tell who had won. As the sun rose, Key saw the gigantic American flag flying over the fort and began writing his poem.

Key's poem has four verses with eight lines each. All four verses make up the national anthem. But today, most people sing only the first verse.

DEFENCE OF FORT M'HENRY.

The annexed song was composed under the following circumstances.— A gentleman had left Baltimore, in a flag of truce for the purpose of getting released from the British fleet, a friend of his who had been captured at Marlborough.—He went as far as the mouth of the Patuxent, and was not permitted to return lest the intended attack on Baltimore should be disclosed. He was therefore brought up the Bay to the mouth of the Patapsco, where the flag vessel was kept under the guns of a frigate, and he was compelled to witness the bombardment of Fort M'Henry, which the Admiral had boasted that he would carry in a few hours, and that the city must fall. He watched the flag at the Fort through the whole day with an anxiety that can be better felt than described, until the night prevented him from seeing it. In the night he watched the Bomb Shells, and at early dawn his eye was again greeted by the proudly waving flag of his country.

Tune—ANACREON IN HEAVEN.

O! say can you see by the dawn's early light,
What so proudly we hailed at the twilight's last gleaming,
Whose broad stripes and bright stars through the perilous fight,
O'er the ramparts we watch'd, were so gallantly streaming?
And the Rockets' red glare, the bombs bursting in air,
Gave proof through the night that our Flag was still there;
O! say does that star-spangled Banner yet wave,
O'er the Land of the free, and the home of the brave?

On the shore dimly seen through the mists of the deep,
Where the foe's haughty host in dread silence reposes,
What is that which the breeze, o'er the towering steep,
As it fitfully blows, half conceals, half discloses?
Now it catches the gleam of the morning's first beam,
In full glory reflected now shines in the stream,
'Tis the star spangled banner, O! long may it wave
O'er the land of the free and the home of the brave.

And where is that band who so vauntingly swore
That the havoc of war and the battle's confusion,
A home and a country, shall leave us no more?
Their blood has washed out their foul footsteps pollution,
No refuge could save the hireling and slave,
From the terror of flight or the gloom of the grave,
And the star-spangled banner in triumph doth wave,
O'er the Land of the Free, and the Home of the Brave.

O! thus be it ever when freemen shall stand,
Between their lov'd home, and the war's desolation,
Blest with vict'ry and peace, may the Heav'n rescued land,
Praise the Power that hath made and preserv'd us a nation!
Then conquer we must, when our cause it is just,
And this be our motto—"In God is our Trust;"
And the star-spangled Banner in triumph shall wave,
O'er the Land of the Free, and the Home of the Brave.

In 1814, "defence" was a common way to spell "defense."

What do Key's words mean to you? Turn the page to take a closer look.

CHAPTER 2

The Star-Spangled Banner

WHAT IT MEANS

The Star-Spangled Banner

O say can you see, by the
dawn's early light,
What so proudly we hail'd at
the twilight's last gleaming?

8

Key asks the question to the two other Americans in the boat with him.

What?

As the sun set last night, the sight of the flag flying over the fort filled us with pride. Now, as the **morning** sun begins to rise over the horizon, is the flag still there? Tell me, can **you** still see it?

The date was September 14, 1814. The night before, Americans had fought the British in the Battle of Baltimore.

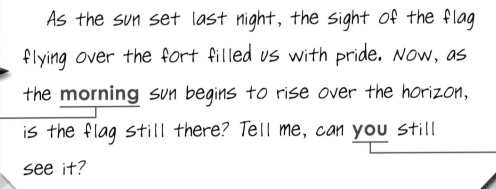

the original flag from Fort McHenry

The Star-Spangled Banner Continued

Whose broad stripes and bright stars, through the perilous fight,
O'er the **ramparts** we watch'd, were so gallantly streaming?

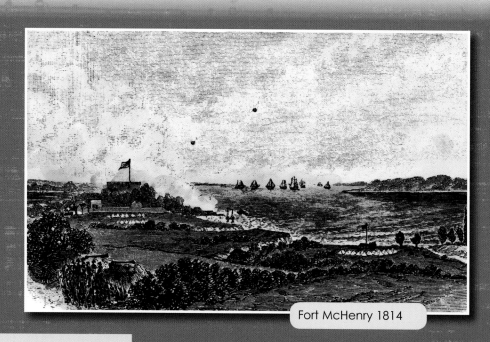

Fort McHenry 1814

rampart — a wall of the fort

British ships fired 1,500 bombshells and 700 rockets at the fort.

What was the fighting about? Turn to page 18 to learn more about the War of 1812.

During last night's **battle**, the British hurled **bomb after bomb** toward **Fort McHenry**. Through it all, we could see the flag's **stars and stripes** flying bravely above the walls of the fort.

Each of the 15 stripes was more than 2 feet (0.6 meters) wide. Each star was twice as large as a human head.

Fort McHenry was built between 1799 and 1802. It protected the city of Baltimore. If the fort fell to the British, Baltimore would also be lost.

Fort McHenry today

11

The Star-Spangled Banner Continued

And the rocket's red glare, the bombs bursting
  in air,
Gave proof through the night that our flag was
  still there.

What?

All night long, bombs blew up overhead, showering sparks onto the water. Meanwhile, **British rockets** zigzagged across the sky. With each flash, we could see **our flag** still flying over the fort. As long as the flag was still there, we knew that the Americans were still in the fight.

If the Americans lost the battle, the British would replace the American flag with one of their own.

British rockets were similar to modern bottle rockets. They left a trail of red light behind them as they flew across the sky.

British flag

13

The Star-Spangled Banner Continued

O say, does that star-spangled banner yet wave
O'er the land of the free and the home of the brave?

Fort McHenry during the battle

What?

Now it is morning. The battle is over. Look again. Is the American flag still flying over the fort? Did our brave soldiers win the fight? Is America still **free**?

The United States had won the Revolutionary War only 31 years earlier. It was now free of foreign rule. Key's words honor those who won that freedom.

And the Rest . . .

What about the rest of the verses? Nobody sings them anymore. But they are still part of the anthem.

In the second verse, Key describes seeing the flag in a beam of morning sunlight. The third verse celebrates that the nation's enemies were driven away. In the last verse, Key thanks God for watching over the country.

The last line of each verse refer to America as the "land of the free and the home of the brave." Key recalls the courage of the patriots who declared independence from Great Britain. They fought bravely to win the Revolutionary War (1775–1783).

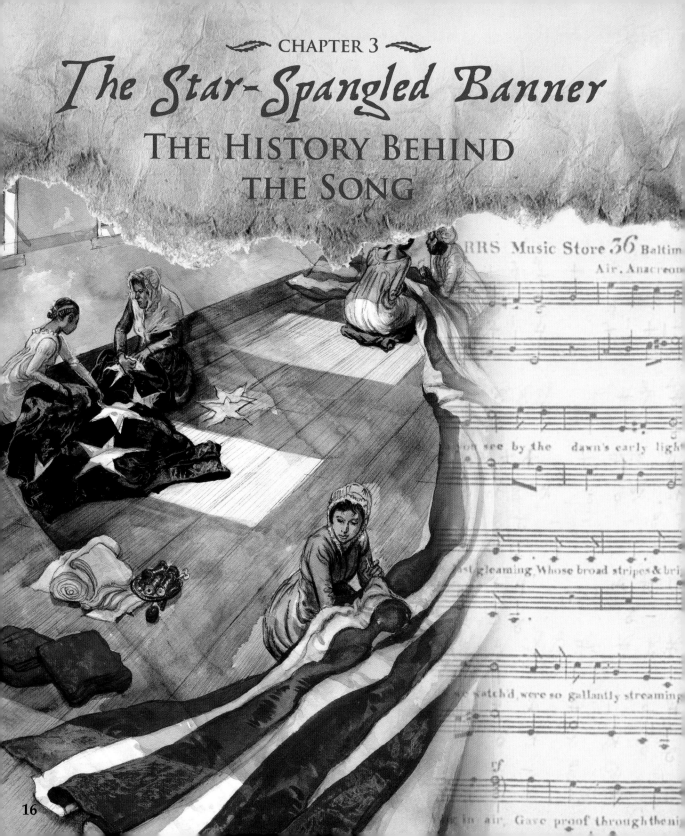

CHAPTER 3

The Star-Spangled Banner
The History Behind the Song

Mary Pickersgill

The Flag

The flag at Fort McHenry was remarkable. In 1813, Major George Armistead became commander at Fort McHenry. He hired Mary Pickersgill, a Baltimore flag maker, to sew two flags for the fort. One would be a smaller flag, called a storm flag. The second flag was going to be huge. He wanted to be sure the British would be able to see it from their ships. Pickersgill asked her 13-year-old daughter, Caroline, and a few others to help make the flags. They sewed both flags by hand. The large flag took more than 350,000 stitches. It measured 30 feet (9 meters) tall by 42 feet (13 meters) wide. Made from 400 yards (366 meters) of wool, the flag weighed at least 80 pounds (36 kilograms).

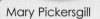

Major George Armistead

The War of 1812

The battle at Fort McHenry took place during the War of 1812. Many Americans called it the Second War of Independence.

For several years, Great Britain and France had been fighting over trade and shipping. The British tried to stop Americans from trading with the French. France was at war with Great Britain. The British seized American ships and cargoes. They also forced American sailors to join the British Navy. Finally, the Americans were fed up. On June 18, 1812, Congress declared war on Great Britain.

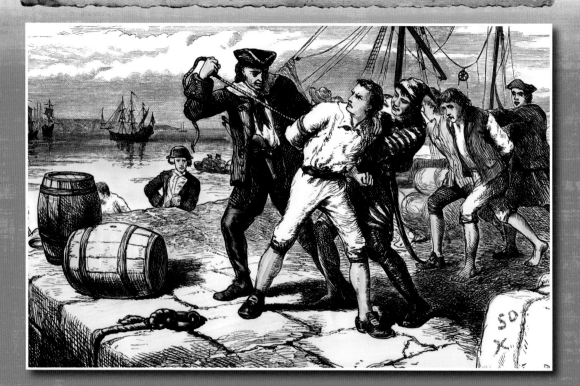

The early battles of the war took place on the border between the United States and Canada. British forces won these battles. Soon the battlefront changed to the Atlantic seacoast. In August 1814, the British Navy landed in Maryland and marched on Washington, D.C. The British destroyed much of the city, burning the White House, the Capitol building, and the Library of Congress. Their next stop was Baltimore, where Fort McHenry stood.

Francis Scott Key

On September 13, 1814, lawyer Francis Scott Key met with General Robert Ross. Ross was the British commander. Key asked Ross to free William Beanes, an American doctor. Beanes was being held prisoner by the British.

Beanes' arrest was a mistake, Key said. The doctor had done nothing wrong. The general agreed, but he couldn't free anybody just then. A battle was about to begin. Key, Beanes, and another American got into a small boat that was tied to a large British ship. They would be allowed to leave when the battle was over.

During the battle, Armistead ordered the fort's giant flag taken down. He feared that the weather and the battle would destroy it. In its place, Armistead raised the storm flag.

Key watched the British attack Fort McHenry from the small boat. The rockets lit up the sky, and Key could see Fort McHenry's flag. If the British won, they would replace the American flag with one of their own. The stars and stripes became a sign of hope.

General Robert Ross

So Was the Flag Still There?

As the sun rose, Armistead ordered the guard to take down the tattered storm flag and raise the giant flag. Through the smoke and fog, Key saw the flag flying over the fort. The Americans had won the battle. In January 1815, the war finally ended.

What Happened to the Giant Flag?

After the battle at Fort McHenry, the fort's commander took the flag home. It stayed with his family until the 1870s. Over the years, some people cut pieces from the flag to keep for themselves. The flag, ripped and worn, was loaned to the Smithsonian Institution in 1907. In 1912, the loan became a permanent gift.

Over the years, experts at the museum preserved and repaired the flag. In 1998, they began an #18 million project to make sure that the flag will last another 200 years. Fort McHenry's giant flag, now called the Star-Spangled Banner, is on display at the Smithsonian in Washington, D.C.

The flag was displayed at Boston Navy Yard in 1874.

The Song

On the morning of September 14, Key began writing "Defence of Fort McHenry" while still in the boat. For paper, he used the back of a letter he had in his pocket. He finished it later in a Baltimore hotel room.

Key wrote out five copies. Each one was just a little bit different. Today, the Library of Congress has one copy. The Maryland Historical Society in Baltimore has another. No one knows what happened to the other three.

Key showed a copy to Judge Joseph H. Nicholson. Nicholson was second-in-command of Fort McHenry. He was so pleased by the poem that he took it to a Baltimore printer and had copies made.

Soon everyone in Baltimore was reading Key's patriotic poem. On September 20, 1814, it appeared in *The Baltimore Patriot* newspaper. It had a new title, "The Star-Spangled Banner." Newspapers around the country reprinted it.

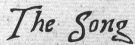

Anacreon Who?

A small note was later added to the printed version of the poem. It pointed out that the words could be sung to a popular tune, "To Anacreon in Heaven."

This song was a theme song of an English men's club. The original words honored Anacreon, a Greek poet who lived around 500 BC. The music was written by London composer John Stafford Smith. During the early 1800s, Smith's tune became popular in Great Britain and America. Several Americans wrote patriotic songs using this tune. Some historians believe Francis Scott Key had this tune in his mind as he wrote the words to his poem.

President Woodrow Wilson

National Anthem

After its early success, the song seemed to disappear. But it came back during the Civil War (1861–1865). Soldiers sang "The Star-Spangled Banner" on their way to battle. It became more popular after the war. By the 1890s, the U.S. Army, Navy, and Marine Corps played it at military events.

In 1916, President Woodrow Wilson declared that "The Star-Spangled Banner" should be played at all government events. People discussed whether it should become the national anthem.

sheet music from 1861

Many people felt that the tune was too hard to sing. Others wanted a gentler song like "America the Beautiful" instead of a song about war. But people in other countries already thought "The Star-Spangled Banner" was the U.S. national anthem. The U.S. Army, Navy, and Marines used it as an anthem. Finally in 1931, Congress made the "The Star-Spangled Banner" the national anthem of the United States.

Both the song and the flag stand for freedom and independence. They remind Americans of the brave people who have served their country.

Time Line

The War of 1812 begins when United States declares war on Great Britain.

Key completes his poem, "Defence of Fort McHenry."

June 1812

September 16, 1814

September 13–14, 1814

1813

September 20, 1814

Major George Armistead hires Mary Pickersgill to sew two flags for Fort McHenry.

The Baltimore Patriot newspaper publishes Key's poem.

Francis Scott Key watches Battle of Baltimore from a boat in the harbor.

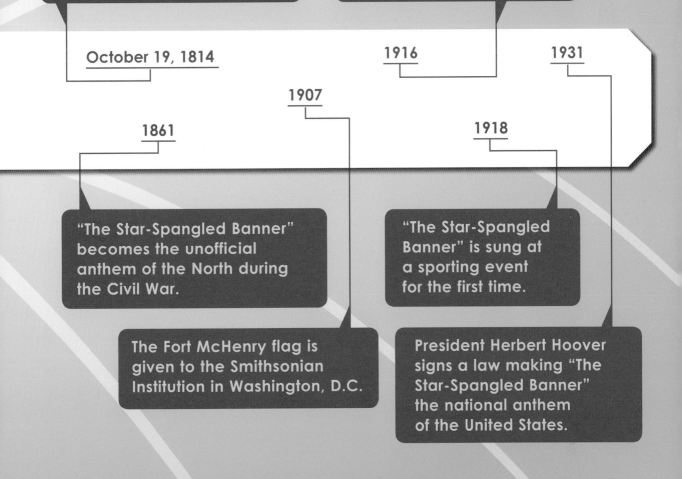

"The Star-Spangled Banner" is performed publicly for the first time in Baltimore to the tune of "To Anacreon in Heaven."

President Woodrow Wilson declares that "The Star-Spangled Banner" should be played at official events.

October 19, 1814

1916

1931

1907

1861

1918

"The Star-Spangled Banner" becomes the unofficial anthem of the North during the Civil War.

"The Star-Spangled Banner" is sung at a sporting event for the first time.

The Fort McHenry flag is given to the Smithsonian Institution in Washington, D.C.

President Herbert Hoover signs a law making "The Star-Spangled Banner" the national anthem of the United States.

Why Do I Care?

5. The song stands for our nation. "The Star-Spangled Banner," like the American flag, is a symbol of our country.

4. Singing "The Star-Spangled Banner" honors the men and women who have served the nation in times of war and in times of peace.

3. Singing our national anthem is a way to honor the president of the United States and members of Congress. The song honors everyone who helps to keep the United States strong and free.

2. The anthem reminds us of the freedoms we enjoy as Americans. We can vote for our leaders, worship as we please, and speak up when we disagree with the government.

1. Respecting the national anthem is the law. The Flag Code says that Americans should stand and remove their hats and face the flag. They should also place their right hands over their hearts whenever the national anthem is played.

gallantly — To be gallant means to be brave and fearless. It also means being worthy of admiration and respect.

hail'd — This was the way Key spelled the word "hailed." He wasn't talking about those small balls of ice that fall from the sky during storms. To hail also means to greet.

o'er — This was a common way to spell "over" in the 1800s.

perilous — Something that is perilous is really, really dangerous.

ramparts — This was just a fancy way of saying the walls of the fort.

rockets — No, there weren't any astronauts at the Battle of Baltimore. Key was talking about weapons similar to modern bottle rockets.

twilight — Twilight is the time of day when the sun sets and it begins to get dark.

Glossary

anthem (AN-thuhm) — a national song

commander (kuh-MAND-ur) — a person in the armed forces who is in charge of other people

horizon (huh-RYE-zuhn) — the line where the sky and the earth or sea seem to meet

independence (in-di-PEN-duhnss) — freedom

lyrics (LIHR-iks) — the words of a song

patriotic (pay-tree-OT-ik) — showing love of and loyalty to one's country

rampart (RAM-part) — the surrounding wall of a fort built to protect against attack

spangle (SPANG-uhl) — a bright decoration

verse (VURSS) — one part of a poem or song made up of several lines

Internet Sites

Use FactHound to find Internet sites related to this book.

Visit **www.facthound.com**

Just type in **9781515791348** and go.

Read More

Alvarez, Pilar. *The War of 1812: New Challenges for a New Nation.* Spotlight on American History. New York: Rosen Publishing, 2017.

Ferris, Mark. *Star-Spangled Banner: The Unlikely Story of America's National Anthem.* Baltimore, Md.: Johns Hopkins University Press, 2014.

Orr, Tamra. *The Star-Spangled Banner.* Mankato, Minn.: Capstone Press, 2006.

Wittekind, Erika. *James Madison's Presidency.* Minneapolis: Lerner Publications, 2016.

Index